What Can We Believe?

Reflections on the Second Readings for Cycle A Proper 23 through Thanksgiving

James L. Killen Jr.

CSS Publishing Co., Inc.
Lima, Ohio

WHAT CAN WE BELIEVE?

FIRST EDITION
Copyright © 2011
by CSS Publishing Co., Inc.

Published by CSS Publishing Company, Inc., Lima, Ohio 45807. All rights reserved. No part of this publication may be reproduced in any manner whatsoever without the prior permission of the publisher, except in the case of brief quotations embodied in critical articles and reviews. Inquiries should be addressed to: CSS Publishing Company, Inc., Permissions Department, 5450 N. Dixie Highway, Lima, Ohio 45807.

Scripture quotations marked (NRSV) are from the New Revised Standard Version of the Bible, copyright 1989 by the Division of Christian Education of the Natioanl Counsil of the Churches of Christ in the USA. Used by permission.

Library of Congress Cataloging-in-Publication Data

Killen, James L.
    What can we believe? : reflections on the second Readings for Cycle A Proper 23 through Thanksgiving / James L. Killen. -- 1st ed.
    p. cm.
    ISBN 0-7880-2631-3 (alk. paper)
    1. Pentecost--Sermons. 2. Bible. N.T. Thessalonians, 1st--Sermons. 3. Thanksgiving--Sermons. 4. Church year sermons. 5. Common lectionary (1992) I. Title.
    BV61.K55 2010
    252'.64--dc22
                           2010040628

ISBN-13: 978-0-7880-2631-7
ISBN-10: 0-7880-2631-3

PRINTED IN USA

To Juanita

What Can We Believe?

Believing is important. We all need to be able to believe that certain big, important, basic things are true and to live as if they are true. Believing is part of putting our lives together so that they will work.

Our Christian faith has taught us some basic beliefs. They are important to us. But in this sophisticated and sometimes cynical age in which we live, many of us are discovering that there are some things people used to believe that we can't believe any more, at least not in the same ways that people used to believe them.

That can be a problem for us. Some of us try to solve the problem by insisting that we are going to keep on believing the things that Christians have always believed — whether or not we can really believe them. That doesn't work very well.

There is another way we can go about solving the problem. We can take a deep, honest look at the great beliefs of the Christian faith and try to understand what they are really all about, and what they really offer to our lives. We can try to distinguish between the message and the envelope. When we do that, we are very likely to discover that the things we can't believe any more are really not the important things, and the important things that the great Christian beliefs have always offered to us are still there for us.

In the series of meditations that follow, we are going to look at some of the great basic teachings of the Christian faith and ask, "What can we believe about that?"

Table of Contents

Proper 23   9
Pentecost 21
Ordinary Time 28
    Can We Believe?
    Philippians 4:1-19

Proper 24   15
Pentecost 22
Ordinary Time 29
    What Can We Believe about the Bible?
    1 Thessalonians 1:1-10

Proper 25   21
Pentecost 23
Ordinary Time 30
    What Can We Believe about the Church?
    1 Thessalonians 2:1-8

Proper 26   29
Pentecost 24
Ordinary Time 31
    What Can We Believe about the Christian Life?
    1 Thessalonians 2:9-13

Reformation Day   37
    What Can We Believe about God's Saving Grace?
    Romans 3:19-28

All Saints   43
    What Can We Believe about Ourselves?
    1 John 3:1-3

Proper 27   **51**
Pentecost 25
Ordinary Time 32
    What Can We Believe about the End of Time?
    1 Thessalonians 4:3-18

Proper 28   **59**
Pentecost 26
Ordinary Time 33
    What Can We Believe about Judgment Day?
    1 Thessalonians 5:1-11

Christ the King   **67**
Proper 29
    What Can We Believe about the Reign of Christ?
    Ephesians 1:15-23

Thanksgiving   **75**
    What Can We Believe about Stuff?
    2 Corinthians 9:6-15

**Proper 23
Pentecost 21
Ordinary Time 28
Philippians 4:1-9**

Can We Believe?

Do you ever find it hard to keep on believing? Do you ever find yourself looking again at the things you always thought were true and wondering, "Can I really still believe that?" Even more importantly, do you ever find it hard to trust?

We all need a basic system of beliefs to help us make sense of the world. We all need to be able to trust something bigger than ourselves so that we can dare to move out into life and live it fully. It is important to be able to believe — but it is not always easy.

We live in a cynical age in where it is more fashionable to doubt than to believe. Modern science — even the modern critical study of the Bible — has called into question some of the things we have always believed. The "in" belief among sophisticated people today is that there are no absolutes. One person's opinion is as good as another and truth is what we decide it is. Besides that, lots of the things we should have been able to trust have let us down lately. You can name them, can't you? When we look carefully at the things people in our culture seem to be clambering after, they seem to be mediocrity advertised with neon signs. In situations like that, it is not always easy to believe.

We might wonder if Paul and the earliest Christians ever had that experience. There is one little word in our epistle reading for today that hints they may have. The word is "if." "If there is any excellence and if there is anything worthy of praise, think about these things" (v. 8).

That little word seems out of place in a letter so full of affirmations. Paul had a very special relationship with the Christians in Philippi. They had shared some very important experiences in faith. Paul believed in their faith. Yet Paul knew that these people lived in a very sophisticated culture where the thinking of people like Plato and Aristotle were still being talked about. Paul had heard that someone had been troubling the Philippians by promoting some kind of an off-brand religion. In addition to that, the church was being churned by a conflict between two of the leading women of the church. That always detracts from the atmosphere of affirmation in a church.

Besides that, Paul himself was not free to go and try to help the people work things out. He was in prison. Being in prison is always a downer. He kept telling himself and everyone else that his imprisonment was going to serve the purpose of his mission. But we can't help wondering if, in the middle of a sleepless night in the prison, Paul himself might have thought he was wasting his life on an illusion. After all, Jesus himself seems to have had some thoughts like that in the Garden of Gethsemane. Could there have been at least a little of an undertow of doubt to Paul's ever-surging tide of faith?

Could Paul have been trying to help the Philippian Christians to keep on believing? If he was, could the things he said to them be helpful to us?

Before we get into what Paul did to help the Philippians believe, we need to think for a while about the dynamics of believing. There are some things we need to keep in mind.

First, it is important to remember that there is more to believing in something than there is in just believing it. It is not enough to just believe intellectually that something is true. If a belief is really going to be allowed to shape your life, there has to be an element of trust in the believing. It is one thing to study the stock market and to believe that a particular stock would be a good investment. It is another thing to invest your life savings in it. It is one thing to believe intellectually that a particular person is a good and admirable person. It is another to marry that person. Believing is more than just thinking something is true.

Believing has to do with something more than just a list of particular beliefs. Our churches teach us some things that we ought to believe. Some churches have a catechism, a list of doctrines that every church member is expected to learn before joining the church. Other churches teach a list of biblical concepts. Churches are not the only ones that want to make contributions to our belief systems. Political parties, unions, fraternal organizations, and cultural traditions offer us teachings to incorporate into our belief systems. All of those specific beliefs are meant to help us see the shape of something bigger. All of them point to some great other. The important thing is for us to find our way into a relationship with that other.

By the way, this business of building a belief system is not just an optional little thing that some people do and others don't. We all live in some kind of a relationship with the great other, and we all develop some kind of a system of beliefs — or doubts — about that other. Some of us do that intentionally. Others of us just drift into it accidentally. We all build some kind of a system of beliefs and, for better or for worse, those beliefs do shape our lives.

If that is what is involved in believing, what did Paul do to help the Philippians believe? The first thing he did — the first thing he always did — was to tell them that God, that great other in relationship with which we all live our lives, was made known to us in Jesus Christ. Jesus was a real person. His life was a real event in human history. For the early Christians it was an event that happened not too long ago. They knew people who had seen it. Paul told them that, in that event, God had shown us what we need to know about

God. God had also shown us what we can and should be as human beings. That was really something amazing.

In the second chapter of his letter, Paul spoke of one who was in the form of God, but did not regard equality with God a thing to be exploited, but emptied himself, "taking the form of a slave, being born in human likeness. And being found in human form, he humbled himself and became obedient to the point of death — even death on a cross" (2:6-8). Paul was telling us that God is one who loves us so much that he sent one who was an aspect of God's own being to take human form and to reach out to us and to become one of us and to suffer for us so that we can find the way into fullness of life. If we can believe that, it means that we can move into life trusting and believing that life is a good gift. Can you see that believing God loves us makes possible a whole new way of life that just is not possible in any other way? Paul told us that we were created to live in self giving love, like God's love, and that the life of love will be life at its best. There you have it in a nutshell. That is the basic belief that should shape the life of one who chooses to be a Christian.

It is no little thing to believe that. It is not always obvious. There are many people who look at all the bad things that happen in life and say you would have to be crazy to believe that life is a gift from someone who loves us. There are those schooled in our culture's way of defensive or exploitative selfishness who would say only a foolish person would live in self-giving love. Yet, that is exactly the belief that shapes a Christian's life. To believe that requires a courageous act of commitment.

That is what it means for us to decide to be Christians. We are called to bet our lives on the belief that the great other out there, the one in relationship with whom we live our lives, is a God who loves us and that the only life that is really worth living is a life of love. Can you believe that?

The Christians at Philippi had made that commitment of faith. However, Paul added some other encouraging suggestions. When you look around at life, you are going to see some things that affirm the revelation of God in Jesus is true and some that seem to deny it. Paul said, focus on the things seen around you that affirm your faith. We can do that too. I am going to read his list over again and as I read, you think of the things you know of in your life that are suggested by the things Paul listed. Are you ready? Let your mind call up pictures of the things these words suggest. Whatever is true — whatever is honorable — whatever is just — whatever is pure — whatever is pleasing — whatever is commendable — if there is any excellence — if there is anything worthy of praise (v. 8). Do you know of things like that in your life and in your world? Those are the things that suggest God actually was made known in Jesus Christ. Think about those things. Hold on to them. Cherish them. They will help you to be able to believe.

The theologian, Paul Tillich, said that it takes courage to venture out into life and to affirm life. He says it is necessary to take an honest look at all of the things that seem to threaten and deny life, to take all of those threats into yourself and move past them in "courage to be." It takes a similar kind of courage to believe. We need to take an honest look at all the things that seem to deny the good news about God's love and then move past them in courage to intentionally believe in spite of all of the evidence to the contrary. One who has courage can dare to believe and to move out to live in faith.

The first American astronauts set an example of what it means to live in faith. Some of them were people of deep religious conviction. They made the venture into space an adventure in faith. In fact, they actually named one of their missions "Faith Seven." One of the most vitally religious of the early astronauts was Ed White. Ed White was the first American to move outside of his space craft and to "walk in space." Sadly, he was also one of the first astronauts to die in the service of the space program. In his memory, a youth center was built at the church he attended. In the youth center is a large-faceted, glass window showing Ed White floating in space, tethered to his space craft only by a thin life line, with the earth in the distance. That window offers us a meaningful image of what it means to believe. It is to move out in courage, past all of the things we are accustomed to depending upon, and to entrust yourself to that great invisible other who is always there.

Can you believe in that way? It may not be easy, but it is possible. If you do that, you may not have answered all of your questions or gotten rid of all of the doubts. But, in the context of a life of faith, you can live with those things and work them out as you have opportunity. The big question about believing is simply this: Can you dare to entrust yourself to the God who was made known in Jesus Christ? Can you let believing what was shown to us in Jesus Christ shape your life?

For those who can, Paul includes a promise among his admonitions. "The peace of God, which surpasses all understanding, will guard your hearts and your minds in Christ Jesus" (v. 7). I wish you that peace. Amen.

Proper 24
Pentecost 22
Ordinary Time 29
1 Thessalonians 1:1-10

What Can We Believe about the Bible?

The words that you have just heard read in our epistle lesson for today are probably the first words that were ever written that became parts of the New Testament. Bible scholars tell us that Paul wrote this letter to the Christians at Thessalonica about twenty years after the death and resurrection of Christ and about twenty years before the Gospel According to Mark was written to collect and preserve the early church's memories of the life of Jesus. This passage can tell us a lot about the Bible as a whole.

The Bible is very important to Christians. It is the source book of our faith. There was a time when Christians reverenced the Bible and studied it as if every single word of it came directly from God. Today, many of us are not sure we can take the Bible that literally. Yet, it is still very important to us. Many of us want to ask, "What can we really believe about the Bible?" Let's explore this first chapter of the letter to the Thessalonians. It will be surprising how much we can learn about the Bible from this one brief passage.

This first chapter is basically the kind of address and greeting that was traditional in personal letters in those days. But Paul enlarged the traditional address. In doing that, he told us many things that we want to know.

The first thing we discover is that when Paul wrote these words, he had no idea he was writing part of the Bible. He was writing a personal letter to some friends who were part of a church Paul and his friends Timothy and Silvanus had helped to bring into being during their missionary work.

He was writing on his own behalf and on the behalf of his coworkers to encourage the church and to renew their witness to the good news of God's love.

We can learn two important things from that. The Bible is a product of the life of the early church. First came the Christ event, God reaching out through Jesus Christ to save. Then came the church, a community of people who had received the good news, accepted God's saving grace, and committed themselves to the purpose of God. Then came the Bible. The New Testament grew up in and through the life of the church over a period of more than 100 years. It was eventually put together in its present form to enable the church to stay in touch with the origin of its faith. Eventually, it came to be regarded as scripture, just like the Hebrew scriptures that were the Bible for the earliest believers.

We can also learn the purpose of Paul's writing. He wrote to make a witness to the saving work of God in Jesus Christ. In fact, all of the writings that were eventually incorporated into both the Old Testament and the New, were written by people who were making their own witness to God. They were all telling what they had learned through their own unique experiences with God.

Were the writings inspired? Indeed they were. In our text, Paul tells us that the Holy Spirit, the presence of the living God, was at work with him and with the church as they grew in their faith. That doesn't mean God dictated the words of the text and Paul wrote them down like a secretary. It means the living God was at work with Paul and with the other Bible writers, and with the members of the early church, and they wrote to tell what they had learned from their interactions with God.

Are any of Paul's human limitations reflected in the Bible? Yes. Paul and the others shared what they had discovered about God as best they could in terms of their own human understanding of reality. In the next chapter, Paul is going to share some personal concerns that he probably would have left out if he had known that he was writing part of the Bible. But that's all right. It simply shows us that the Christian faith is rooted in real human life just like our own. A little later in our study of 1 Thessalonians, we are going to discover that when Paul wrote this book, he was still expecting Jesus would return and bring in the kingdom of God within the next few years. That didn't happen. But that's all right. It simply helps us to know that our understanding of the saving work of God has to keep on growing like Paul's did.

The important thing is still there. The Bible writers had experienced the reality of God and they were writing to tell about it. The Holy Spirit was at work in their lives and in their witness.

In these verses, Paul also says something else that is often overlooked. He says to the Thessalonians, "... you received the word with joy inspired by the Holy Spirit" (v. 6). Those who receive the word should be open to the work of the Holy Spirit. That means we ought to be open to the work of the Holy Spirit as we read the biblical witnesses. That doesn't have to mean anything spooky. It simply means that when we read the Bible, we should do so remembering the God about whom the Bible writers wrote is still God, and the biblical witnesses can lead us into our own personal relationships with the living God. That is really what the Bible is for.

This brief introduction to Paul's letter actually includes an amazing amount of Paul's own understanding of the Christian faith. Let's look at some of the things he said.

He starts with the greeting, "To the church of the Thessalonians in God the Father and the Lord Jesus Christ" (v. 1). For Paul, God, the God who was present in Jesus Christ and with whom Jesus Christ is present now, is the very context of our existence. It is a little misleading to think of them being "in heaven" as we traditionally have. Now, in this space age, we know we cannot think of heaven as a place on the other side of the sky. God and the Lord Jesus Christ are with us everywhere. They are present with us wherever we are. They come to meet us in our daily interactions with life.

Then Paul gives a traditional greeting, "Grace to you and peace" (v. 1). The concept of grace is the pivotal center of Paul's understanding of God's way of relating to us. Grace means the freely given love of God for us. It is through the working of God's love in our world and in our lives that we have hope of salvation, both in this world and beyond it. Peace is the kind of wholeness that God can bring into our lives through his grace.

Next, Paul says something that is a summary of his understanding of the way in which we should respond to God's freely given love. He says he remembers before God in prayer the Thessalonian's works of faith, labors of love, and steadfastness in hope in our Lord Jesus. Later, Paul will end his very special chapter on love, 1 Corinthians 13:13, by saying, "Now faith, hope, and love abide, these three, and the greatest of these is love."

Faith is basic trust. It is taking God's love in and letting it shape your life. It is learning to relate to both God and life on the basis of trust. In the letter to the Ephesians (2:8), there is a summary of Paul's gospel that says, "... By grace you have been saved through faith."

Love is the shape of the life to which God wants to save us. Love is a joyful commitment of life to life. In its most mature form, it is a joyful commitment to the life and well being of self, of God, and of all that God loves.

Hope is the kind of expectancy that comes from knowing God is at work in our world and in our lives. It keeps us always open to life.

It is interesting that Paul has hidden in this earliest writing the answer to a dispute that would arise in the church much later, probably after Paul had died. Late in the history of the church, some people came to believe that salvation by faith means we are saved by being religious or by making a profession of faith. The epistle of James challenged that idea by saying, "Show me your faith apart from your works, and I by my works will show you my faith" (James 2:18). Paul would have agreed completely. When he spoke of faith, Paul was not talking about formal religion. He was talking about a whole way of living in relationship with God and with life, something that will shape a person's life and works. In these earliest verses, Paul spoke of "works of faith and labors of love."

Here we have a summary of Paul's witness to the saving work of God. There are other witnesses in the Bible. Paul speaks of "grace" and "faith." The writers of the Hebrew scriptures spoke of God working in history to save the people, or of God making a covenant, or of God demanding justice. In the New Testament, we will hear Matthew making his witness by talking about "the kingdom of God" and John making his by talking about "eternal life." Other Bible writers make their own unique witnesses to the saving work of God as they experienced it. What is this? Are there conflicts in the Bible? Not important ones. We have different witnesses telling about their own unique experiences with God in their own special ways. It is as if each of the biblical witnesses is describing a mountain from a different point of view so that we can get the whole picture. The reality they are describing is not something inert like a mountain. It is something alive and in interaction with the people who make their witness. All together, they show us how many possibilities there are for us when we enter into a personal relationship with the living God.

That brings us to one last thing that our chapter tells us about the Bible… its purpose. The Bible is not given to us to give us information, even though we have been mining it for information and digging out a lot of it. It is not meant to just answer puzzling questions about theology, let alone about history or science. It is given to us to lead us into a personal relationship with God that will change our lives and make us agents of God to change the world. Paul makes it clear that is what was happening in and among the Christians at Thessalonica.

Once a very intelligent and very cynical young college student by the name of Anthony Bloom was persuaded by the leaders of his youth organization to go to a meeting at which a certain minister was to be the speaker. He didn't want to go. He was finally persuaded that he should go because they didn't want to be embarrassed by a small turn out to hear a guest speaker. The minister's presentation did nothing to improve Anthony's opinion. In fact, his impression was so repulsive that he decided to get a Bible and read one of the gospels just to convince himself once and for all that there is nothing to the Christian faith. He chose Mark because it is the shortest of the gospels. The results were not what he expected. He said he had no sooner begun to read than he became aware of a presence standing there just beyond his reading table. He said, "... the certainty was so strong that it was Christ standing there that it has never left me."[1] He became a Christian and a leader in his church. Eventually, he became an Archbishop of the Orthodox church and one who led many others into vital relationships with God. That can happen. The Bible was given to us to help us discover God in our lives and in our world. That can make a big difference.

What can we believe about the Bible? It is the collection of the witnesses of the members of the community of faith to their interactions with the living God. It is given to us to lead us into our own interaction with God. And that can lead us to the life that really is life. Amen.

---

1. Anthony Bloom, *Beginning to Pray* (New York: Paulist Press, 1970), pp. 9-10.

**Proper 25
Pentecost 23
Ordinary Time 30
1 Thessalonians 2:1-8**

What Can We Believe about the Church?

What can we believe about the church? That is an important question for us to ask and to answer. An awful lot of people today have a very low opinion of the church. Many people think that it is, at best, unimportant and unnecessary, and at worst, something that is a real hindrance to everything good. You have heard them. Some say, "I am a spiritual person and I believe that Jesus was a great teacher, but I don't want to have anything to do with organized religion." Others delight in cataloging all of the failures of the church and its people so they can feel righteous about not going to church.

Our scripture lesson makes it clear that Paul had a very different attitude toward the church. He was deeply committed to the church. He was committed to spreading the Christian gospel and building up the church in spite of the hardship and persecution he had to endure to do it. When Paul first came to Thessalonica to preach, he had just come from Philippi where he had a bad experience. It seems that there was some opposition at Thessalonica too. But in spite of all of that he came and preached the gospel boldly. He was committed.

Paul was also very careful to maintain his personal integrity for the sake of the church. Apparently there were already some religious teachers who were exploiting the people who were drawn to them. (Some things don't change.) Paul reminded the people that he was not one of those. It would have been perfectly appropriate for Paul to have received a salary for the work he did. But he chose not to so that there would be no question about his motives.

Most important of all, Paul related himself to the church in love. He came representing the God who loves us. He came teaching the people a life of love. So he related himself to the people and to the church in Thessalonica in love. They knew that he loved them. He said, "So deeply do we care for you that we are determined to share with you not only the gospel of God, but also our own selves, because you have become very dear to us" (v. 8).

Why did Paul feel that way about the church? It was because of what he believed about the church.

Paul had no illusions about the church. He knew well the humanity of the church. As we read all of the letters of Paul, we find he had to deal with all of the shortcomings and failures and temptations that churches have to reckon with today. Yes, Paul knew about the humanity of the church.

However, Paul believed that the church is more than a human institution. He believed that the church is of God. In the addresses of his letters to the church at Corinth, he spoke of them as "The church of God in Corinth" (1 Corinthians 1:2 and 2 Corinthians 1:1). He believed that the church is part of God's plan and that God is present and at work in and through the church.

In the first of those letters, he spells out his belief about the church. He calls it the body of Christ (1 Corinthians 12). The image of the church suggests two things. One is that the church is made up of many different people with different talents and functions who work together like the different parts of a human body with Christ as the head. It also suggests that the church is a body of people to whom God has entrusted the mission of carrying on the work God was doing in the world through Jesus Christ.

What is that work? To give the world hope. To enable the world to trust. To teach the world to love. In that way, God can use the church to save the world from all the things that distort and destroy life in its fullness.

Does the world need that? Look around.

Look around at all of the fear, hate, and conflict in our world. Look at the wars and the terrorism, the tyranny and the other forms of violence that are always waiting, threatening to break out and tear our world apart. Remember that the threat of nuclear war or nuclear terrorism is not gone.

Look at the communities and families being torn apart or kept in crippling tension because of deep conflicts and mistrust. Look at the structures of business, industry, and community life that are falling apart because of a loss of integrity. Look at our inability to trust the things we ought to be able to trust.

Look at all of the human suffering in our world, the results of wars, displacement, and exploitation. Look at the widespread poverty in our world. One sixth of the world's people are malnourished. Thirty-six million people, including thirteen million children, in the United States live in homes where there is not enough to eat.[1] There is something wrong with a world like that. What would it take to fix it?

Take a closer look. There are some things that your pastor knows that you probably don't know. He knows how much suffering there is among the people who live on your block, the people whose children go to school with yours, and the people you see standing in the line at the grocery store. Most of us don't see the amount of marital stress, the child or spousal abuse, the clinical depression, the addictions, the growing desperation, the inclination toward suicide that are all around us. But they are there. What will it take to fix that?

Take an even closer look. Look within your own life. Is your own life all that it could be? Is it all that you want it to be?

When we look at needs like that we ask what it would take to fix them. We are accustomed to thinking first about some change in the circumstances of our lives and of our world, something to which we could probably assign a value in terms of dollars. And those things are important. Before we come to those things, there are some even more basic needs that cry out to be met.

There is a need to be able to rise above discouragement and despair and take hold of hope, a need to believe that something really good can happen.

There is a need to be able to relate to life in basic trust, to see behind all of the things that disappoint us, something greater that will always be there for us, something that loves us, something in which we can have faith.

Most of all, when we have taken hold of hope and learned to trust, we need to be able to move out into life in love, in a basic commitment of our lives to all of life, a willingness to give ourselves to the well being of our own lives and the lives of others and the life of the creation as a whole.

If those intangible things are alive and at work in our lives, in our communities, and in our world, they will make the differences that need to be made in the lives of the people who are hurting. Eventually, they will change those circumstances that are hurtful to human life.

Where do hope and trust and love come from? If we believe the Christian gospel, we believe that God is at work in our world and in our lives to make those things happen. That is an important part of what it means that God is at work in our lives and in our world to save us. Yes, salvation does have to do with a hope that reaches beyond this life. It also has to do with something God is doing to make a difference in our world and in our lives in the here and now. And the beginning of that saving work is in the growth of hope, of faith, and of love.

Where does God do that saving work? Everywhere. God is not limited. God works through families, community agencies, friendship groups, and political action groups. God works through all of the great religions of the world. But we believe that God has made his saving work known to us most perfectly in Jesus Christ. There is only one agency in the world that is intentionally and completely committed to doing the work of Christ, only one agency in the whole world has taken that as its primary purpose. That is the church. The primary purpose for which the church exists addresses the deepest and most basic needs of humanity in this world. It addresses our own most basic needs too.

So, is the church important? Those people who say they don't want to have anything to do with "organized religion" are either deeply disillusioned or they have just chosen other purposes for their lives and don't want to be bothered with anything that doesn't serve that purpose. If we recognize that the deepest needs of the world can be best met by what the Christian faith has to offer, then we will know that those who believe will need to get organized to offer the world what it needs to keep it from dying — or self-destructing.

Paul saw that and that is why he related himself to the church as he did. Can we see that? If we do, how should we relate ourselves to the church? If we follow Paul's example, our response will have to take the shape of commitment. Commitment is not a very popular thing in our culture. That is part of what is wrong with our culture. A call to commitment is part of what our faith offers us for our salvation. Love is really a matter of commitment. Love is the main thing most of us need to make our lives into real life. Committing ourselves to something greater than ourselves can make us bigger people. Our commitment must be to God and to all that God is doing in our lives and in our world. That commitment will have to be invested in lots of different ways. But part of our commitment to God will certainly have to be invested in the church, the agency on earth to which God has entrusted the work he began in Christ.

What shape should our commitment to the church take? It can start by taking the shape of expectancy. Paul didn't say anything about it in today's passage of scripture, but he must have looked to the church for the nurturing of his own faith. He must have remembered Barnabas and the other members of the early church who took him under their wings and shared the faith with him. He must have been fed spiritually by his relationships with the Christians in Thessalonica and in all of the other churches with which he worked.

We will do the church a service by going to the church to have our own spiritual needs met. Yes, that can sometimes set us up for disappointment. But, what would happen if you would speak up someday in Sunday school and say, "I have come here hoping to be saved. I have come here hoping to get hold of some hope, hoping to learn to be able to trust, and hoping to learn to live in love"? The expectation just might bring about some real spiritual renewal in your congregation.

Then, insofar as you can, by expectation and by action, you should work to build up the integrity of the church. When we get honest about things, we have to recognize that the church has not always lived up to its highest calling. Some people say that the church has become so preoccupied with its own institutional success that it has forgotten its mission. That is certainly something that has been a temptation for the church in every age. If you are a member of the church, a functioning part of it, you can work to keep that from happening. We all should.

Finally, your commitment to the church must take the shape of love. That was really Paul's most important commitment. The Christian faith is about love. It is about God loving us into the ability to love as God loves. That is what should be going on in the church and through the church in the world. Love is a giving of self, a commitment of life to life. Paul said, "So deeply do we care for you that we are determined to share with you not only the gospel of God but also our own selves, because you have become very dear to us" (v. 8). The more we do that, the more the church will really be the body of Christ that God calls it to be.

So now look around you. Where are we? We are in church, aren't we? This is the building we have been accustomed to calling the church. These people around us are the people we have been accustomed to calling our church. We have been doing the things we are accustomed to doing in church. We see around us the things about our church that have sometimes annoyed us — and also the things about our church that we have always loved. Here we are in church. And we have been talking about what it means to be church. So let's do it. Amen.

---

1. George McGovern, Bob Dole, Donald E. Messer, *Ending Hunger Now* (Minneapolis: Fortress Press, 2005), pp. viii-ix.

Proper 26
Pentecost 24
Ordinary Time 31
1 Thessalonians 2:9-13

What Can We Believe about the Christian Life?

Paul frequently reminded the Thessalonians of the kind of life that he and his friends lived while they were with them. He also reminded them that they had dealt with them like a father with his children, urging and encouraging them and pleading that they should "lead a life worthy of God, who calls you into his own kingdom and glory" (v. 12). Later in the same chapter, Paul recognizes that the Christians in Thessalonica had indeed lived lives following the example of other Christians, even though it had been costly for them to do so. It is important for Christians to live a Christian life.

We all believe that. We have a very low opinion of anyone who claims to be a Christian and does not live a Christian life. But what is a Christian life? Most of us have an idea of the Christian life that is pretty bland: be a nice person and a good neighbor, stay out of trouble, follow the ten commandments, go to church, and do something good for someone else now and then. We assume that a person who lives that kind of life will go to heaven when he or she dies. Most of us have an idea of the Christian life that is pretty much like that. And it is really not very exciting, is it? To tell the truth, we have purposefully set the bar pretty low. We don't want too much to be expected of us. We really don't want to be asked to be very different from everyone else.

But, when we read the Bible, we get a very different idea of what it means to live the Christian life, one that is more demanding, more risky, more exciting, and more likely to lead to a really extraordinary existence. Then what can we believe about the Christian life? You know there is no way we can answer that question in twenty minutes. We can at least outline some of the characteristics of a Christian life. Let's try.

First, the Christian life is the prize, not the prerequisite. Lots of people still think living the Christian life is something you have to do to qualify to go to heaven after you die. In fact, the Christian life here and now is the prize; not the prerequisite. A hope that reaches beyond death is part of the Christian life but the gift of God starts here and now. Each of us has only one life to live in this world, and we want to make the most of it. We want to live life at its best. Unfortunately, most of us have allowed the advertising industry to create our image of the good life. They would have us scrambling after materialistic prizes designed to make someone else rich. People who spend their one life perusing that goal are likely to be disappointed and disillusioned. God has something for us that is much better. It is a better way of putting life together. It results in a new quality of life. It is not something for which you have to qualify. God has put it there for you. You just have to take it up and live it. Jesus said the new life of the kingdom of God is like a treasure hidden in a field. When you trip over it and realize what you have found, you will be willing to sell everything else that you have in order to possess it (Matthew 13:44).

The Christian life is a life organized around a relationship; not around rules. Yes, there are rules, the ten commandments, the sermon on the mount, and others. They are helpful when we have decisions to make. We ignore them at our own peril. But they really point beyond themselves to something else. The Christian life is a life organized around a relationship with God. If you are married, you know how a relationship can shape your life. Your relationship with one very important other person can shape your life from the inside out. It can influence everything from the way you feel about yourself to the way you dress. When Paul spoke of the life of the kingdom of God, he was talking about a life in which God is the most important other in your life and in which your relationship with God shapes your life. Jesus said, "No one can serve two masters..." (Matthew 6:24). The Christian life is a life that is being shaped by a relationship with God.

The Christian life is an adventure because the God in relationship with whom we are living our lives is alive and at work in exciting and unpredictable ways. The writers of the Hebrew scriptures tell us about a God who worked in human history to save his people from slavery in Egypt and to make them into a special people. The writers of the gospels tell about a God who came among us in the person of one like ourselves to show us God's love and to open to us a new possibility. The writers of Acts and the epistles tell us about a God who continued to be at work in the lives of all who would be open to him to bring them to wholeness and to send them out to change the world. To live in relationship with that God is to try to discover what God is doing in your life and in your world and live in responsiveness to it. To live in relationship with a God like that is sure to be an adventure. It is like paddling a canoe in a rapid river. You are living in relationship with one who is alive. When Jesus came to those whom he wanted to be his disciples, he said, "Follow me." He was indeed calling them into an adventure. It takes courage to venture out into that kind of a life, but courage is rewarded with expectancy. The Christian life is not dull. It is an adventure.

The Christian life takes a unique shape in each unique person and in each unique community. The Christian faith is not like a "one size fits all" garment. It is like a garment tailor made to fit your own size and character. God reaches out to you where you are in life and interacts with you in ways that are appropriate to your unique needs and possibilities and to your unique situation in life. When God goes to work in your life, God does not make you into someone other than yourself. God makes you the very best you that you can be. But there are some experiences that many Christians have had that you may experience in your own way as you let your life be shaped by your relationship with God.

The Christian life often starts with a joyful discovery that God loves you. Some people grow up knowing that God loves them. They are the lucky ones. Others have to discover it for themselves. Jesus came to show us God's love for us. It is not a love we have to earn. It is freely given. We can see evidences of God's love for us in everything good and beautiful. We can see it especially in human love. All real love comes from God and brings God's love to us. Some of us discover God's love for us when we are feeling guilty, beaten, or good for nothing. In situations like that discovering we are loved by the one who is the most important other that there is can make a big difference in our lives. It can help us to know ourselves to be forgiven, accepted, healed, respected, valued, liberated, and enabled. The knowledge of the love of God is really good stuff. It is miraculous stuff. In one way or another, it needs to be a part of every Christian's life. It is there for you. If you are not experiencing it, reach out for it. And keep on reaching out. It is an important part of what God wants to do in your life.

The Christian life is shaped by many different kinds of interactions with the living God. God keeps on reaching out to us and interacting with us through our interactions with life. The Bible writers tell stories about things God did in their lives to meet their unique needs. Some who were bewildered about the meaning of life, spoke of Christ coming to them as a "Word" that helped them understand what life is all about. Some who were sunk in hopelessness, spoke of Christ coming as a Messiah who offered them a new possibility. Some who had messed their lives up recognized God working in the failures and frustrations of their lives to show them that they needed to make some changes. Some who were drifting and living purposeless lives told of one who was a servant of God who came calling them to be servants of God too. Some who felt overwhelmed by the thought of living the Christian life in a strange and hostile world spoke of Jesus as the pioneer of their faith who lived the Christian life before them to show them how to do it and that it can be done. All of these tell how God worked in their lives to save and to make them whole. God is still working in all of these ways and in others that are appropriate to your own needs. It is important for you to know well the stories about what God has done so that you can recognize what God may be doing in your interactions with life. Then you can open yourself to what God is doing and respond in ways that will allow God to change your life. But where is all of this going? What is the shape of the life toward which God is moving us?

    The Christian life is a life lived in love. That is the basic shape of it. Jesus said, "... you shall love the Lord your God with all your heart, with all your soul, and with all your mind, and with all your strength." And, "You shall love your neighbor as yourself. There is no other commandment greater than these" (Mark 12:30-31). In another place, he said that we are to love as God loves (Matthew 5:43-48). That is the shape of the Christian life. But the love Jesus was talking about in not just a warm fuzzy thing. It is something substantial and capable of making a difference. You know the text that says, "For God so loved the world that he gave his only Son, so that everyone who believes in him may not perish but may have eternal life" (John 3:16). The love referred to in that verse has to be a deep commitment of life to life, the kind of commitment that will make a person do what is best for the one who is loved no matter what the cost.

It is a joyful commitment of life to life. God loves us with that kind of love and God wants us to love ourselves with that kind of love too. That is an important first step. God loves us and God wants us to love ourselves as God loves us. Then God wants us to enlarge the circle of our love so that we will also love others, all others, all that God loves. That is what it means to love God with our whole being. How can we do that? God will love us into being able to do that. If we will live in openness to God in all of our relationships, God will love us into loving as God loves. Even though we may never have thought of it, the life of love is really the life that we all yearn for, the treasure hidden in a field. A once popular song said, "What the world needs now is love sweet love. That's the only thing that there's just too little of." It is to the life of love that God works to save us. It is the most precious thing of all. It is the life worthy of God who calls you into his kingdom and glory.

The Christian life is a life that makes things different. It will make you different. It has always been a mistake to want to be just like everyone else. To do that is to sacrifice the real value of God's gift. No, it is not necessary to strut around acting superior and making others uncomfortable. But the difference is real and profound. Do you remember the beatitudes with which Jesus began the sermon on the mount? "Blessed are the poor in spirit, for theirs is the kingdom of heaven. Blessed are those who mourn, for they shall be comforted. Blessed are the meek, for they will inherit the earth" (Matthew 5:3-5) and the others. These describe the life of a person that has been totally reorganized from the inside out, so that he or she finds blessedness and happiness in the places where no one else would ever think to look for it. The Christian life will make other people differently. If you relate yourself to everyone whom you know in a love like God's love, your love will bear God's love to others, and that will make a great and joyful difference in their lives. If you move into the life of the world and live there a life that is shaped by love that will make a difference. Some people may not like it because they may not understand it. For that reason, it can be costly to live the life of love. It was for Jesus. But people living the life of love in the world will ultimately change the world and make it what God created it to be. Jesus said, "The kingdom of heaven is like yeast that a woman took and mixed with three measures of flour until all of it was leavened" (Matthew 13:33). Living the Christian life makes things different.

What can we believe about the Christian life? We have used lots of words to try to answer. But you can only discover the shape of the Christian life when you dare to venture out to try to live it. Paul said he was grateful when the Thessalonians heard his words, they heard the word of God coming through them. Then he said that the word of God was at work among those who believed, at work to make a difference, at work to save (v. 13). That can happen for you if you will let it. Amen.

Reformation Day
Romans 3:19-28

What Can We Believe about God's Saving Grace?

The grace of God is the theme of some of our favorite hymns. "Amazing grace, how sweet the sound," "Grace, grace, God's grace, grace that is greater than all of our sins." We know this is an important Christian doctrine. It is the primary thrust of the teaching of Paul. It was the pivotal doctrine of the Protestant Reformation. We know the words, "By grace you are saved through faith." But what does it mean? It is not enough to have heard of grace. We need to have experienced it. And in order to experience grace, we have to experience our need for grace. Today, we are going to dig into the meaning of the text that is the very center of Paul's theology. But to understand Paul's theology, we need to go behind it and remember Paul's experience — and to think about its similarity to our own experience. Today we are going deep. What can we really believe about God's saving grace?

Some of us need grace because we feel that we are not acceptable. We feel that we have not measured up to expectations. Christianity is a religion of high expectations. So was the religion of the Pharisees, the strict form of Judaism in which Paul grew up. High expectations are good. They play an important role in our lives. But they are only part of what we need. If the high expectations are all that we have, they can be oppressive. Paul felt this very painfully. In Romans 7, he tells us that he knew he could never really live up to the expectations of his religion. He would never really be the person the Jewish religious laws wanted him to be, at least not alone.

Not many people today are that oppressed by the requirements of their religion. Frankly, most of us don't take it that seriously. There are other expectations that can become oppressive. The things that our parents expect of us and the success that our culture tells us we must achieve to be considered a person of worth. When we are young, it may be the expectations of the little league coach or the expectations of the teen peer group. What is it for you? What are the expectations that have made you feel like a failure?

A man who grew up in Singapore once told his American pastor something very revealing. He said he admired the Christian church in Singapore for their success in suicide prevention. The pastor asked what he meant and the man explained that the educational system in Singapore is the old British system. Students in school have to pass certain examinations at crucial times in their education or they will be dropped out of the system. Their professional and social possibilities will then be limited for the rest of their lives. In Chinese families, the pressure to succeed is so great that, if a young person fails one of those examinations, he or she may feel that he or she has let the family down. After those examinations, there is always a wave of suicides among young people who feel disgraced and see no reason for going on. The Christian church in Singapore has developed effective ways of reaching out to those people and convincing them that God still loves them, that they do still have value as people, and that life still has possibilities for them.

It may be that your need for an experience of grace takes a shape like that. Do you feel that you have not measured up? Do you ever feel that life is a great party but you did not qualify for an invitation? That may be the need that makes you stand in need of an experience of God's grace.

For some of us, there is something bigger. The first time Paul appeared in the Bible's story, he was an ambitious young Pharisee named Saul who stood and watched a mob stone Stephen to death for witnessing to the saving grace of God in Christ. Stephen had been sentenced to death by stoning by the Jewish authorities. Paul stood and watched and cheered while Stephen prayed for those who were killing him. The stones finally crushed his skull and he died. For some people there is something attractive and contagious about hatred. Paul jumped on the bandwagon. He got himself deputized to search out and arrest all of the Christians he could find and take them to prison. He threw himself into that work with a vengeance, but apparently the memory of Stephen being stoned stayed with him. As he was on his way to Damascus to do his awful work, it all finally caught up with him. He heard the risen Christ saying, "Saul, what are you doing?" Then he was struck blind so he would have time to think about it.

Is there some memory of something you have done or participated in doing that really haunts you? Can you remember a time when you failed to give a loving response when it was needed and caused suffering for another? Is there something that your circumstances require of you that you know really is not right, maybe at work, maybe in the family? Is there something that happened during a war that you can't forget? Has there been an abortion — or a divorce — or a lie that haunts you? You have to fill in the blank here. What is that memory that just won't leave you alone?

There are two kinds of public enemies that I think we need to avoid as we think about this. One is the bombastic preacher who spends all of his time trying to make people feel guilty so he can sell you his little prepackaged plan of salvation. The other is the spokesman of our permissive culture who tells you there is no such thing as guilt. You can do whatever you want, whatever is profitable or pleasurable, and not worry about the consequences, either for yourself or for others. That sounds attractive, but it is like a friend who urges you not to get your cancer treated. You know the thing that haunts you is serious because it has let someone down or done some damage or at least subtracted something from the integrity of the human race. I am going to count on you to fill in the blank here. Each of you will know what we are talking about. If you don't, just remember what we are going to say in case you do eventually find that you need it.

As we said, Paul's guilt finally caught up with him on the road to Damascus, and he was left for a time to reckon with it. Then a courageous little man by the name of Ananias came to him and said, "Brother Saul, God sent me to tell you that God loves you and that he has something good for you to do." The story goes on from there.

In our scripture lesson for today, we have heard a piece of the theology that Paul finally developed to try to explain what God is doing to save us. He talks about the atonement. Now I know that some people think this is the whole story of the saving work of God. It is not. The biblical witness to the saving work of God talks about different ways in which God reaches out to people in need and works to save them. But this is one of the important witnesses to the saving work of God, the one that has to do with guilt, and that is what we are talking about right now. So let's try to hear the message. Paul talks about the atonement, the idea that Christ died to pay the cost of our sins. Now lots of people have trouble with some of the things that seems to imply, such as the idea that God insists someone has to suffer for any sinfulness. I have some trouble with that idea too. But it is really not important. It is part of the stage settings for the real drama. It is best to forget that and move directly to the bottom line. What is this biblical witness to the saving work of God trying to tell us?

Here it is. Our sins are serious. They are serious because they are destructive. But God has absorbed the costs that result from our wrongness and God sets those things aside and forgives us. God loves you. God loves you right now, just as you are. God is reaching out to you in love, in many different ways, to work with you and to help you get your life together and make it something beautiful and genuinely good. That's it in a nutshell. Now let's look at it part by part.

There is a cost to our wrongness. Deep down inside, we know that. It is costly not just because we have broken some moral law. It is costly because it has done damage to some other person or to the very structure of life in human society or to ourselves. It is the destructiveness that gets something on God's list of "Thou shalt nots" and not just someone's puritanical uptightness. God and the whole of human society has absorbed that cost. It hurt but it was done. The image of Christ suffering on the cross to pay the price for our sins is a meaningful one. Our wrongness is costly — but it is forgiven.

When the people of South Africa decided that they had to move out of the era of oppression called apartheid into a new era of democracy, they knew they had to reckon with the enormous amount of harm that had been done by people on all sides of the conflict. People had been arrested and held in prison for years. People had been evicted from their homes. People had been tortured and killed. People had been necklaced with old tires and burned to death. It just would not be possible to act as if those things hadn't happened. But then, neither was it possible to punish all for the crime. There was too much of it. Too many people had been dragged into it. They would have to forgive in order to move on. First they had to call their sin what it was and admit it and repent of it. They actually found a way of doing that as a nation. They called it the Truth and Reconciliation Commission. The nation absorbed the painful things that had happened in the past so they could move on. God has made the same decision about our sins. God absorbs them so we can move on.

Can you take that in? God has absorbed the cost of whatever it is that is haunting you so you can leave it behind and move on.

Now we have come to the starting place. Lots of people think that having your sins forgiven is the end of the process of salvation, but it is not. It is the starting place. Having been set free from what was, you are ready to move on toward what can be.

The first part of what comes next is the news that God loves you. Do you know what that means? Lots of people have never really experienced love. To be loved is to be valued by another, not for what you can do, but for yourself. When someone loves you, that someone makes a commitment to your life, wants what is best for you, and is willing to do whatever is necessary to help you reach what is best for you, even if doing it is costly. Do you know that kind of love? I hope you do. The good news is that God, that great other who is ultimately the most important other in the world, loves you with that kind of love.

God is ready to enter into a lifelong, life-shaping relationship with you to help you become all that you can become. One person who is active in Alcoholics Anonymous is fond of saying, "God loves us just as we are. But he loves us too much to leave us just as we are." When you take God as your partner in living, life will become an adventure in becoming and it will be full of exciting possibilities.

It is not pleasant to talk about our need for salvation. It makes it necessary to remember things we have been trying to forget. But there is something better than just forgetting. I hope this hasn't been too painful for you. I just want to be for you an Ananias who comes to say, Brother Saul, Sister Jane, Brother Bill, God loves you and God has something better in store for you. Amen.

All Saints
1 John 3:1-3

What Can We Believe about Ourselves?

When we put together the collection of things that we can believe, we need to ask a question about the person in the middle of the inquiry. What can we believe about ourselves? We don't often ask that question but it is a very important one. Some people are oppressed by low self-esteem. Others are led astray by exaggerated images of themselves. It is important to get a realistic understanding of who we are — and of who we can be. The Bible has something to say on the subject that may surprise you. Are you ready? Hold on to your hat. The Bible says you were created and called to be saints. In fact, in the eyes of God, that is who you are.

Most of us want to start kicking and screaming when we hear that suggestion. Most of us don't think we ever could be saints even if we wanted to — and we don't. The Bible does tell us that is our heritage. Since this is All Saints' Day, let's ask what the Bible means by that.

Who are the saints of God? When we think of saints, we usually think of the apostles and martyrs from the past whose stone statues greet us in church yards or stand in alcoves around the walls of great cathedrals, gazing through sightless eyes at the people who come to worship. But when we read the biblical stories of the people represented by those statues, we learn that they were not images carved in stone at all. They were real people, people like us in every way, warts and all, who had made a discovery that brought them to life in a new way and set them to growing and serving and being all that they were created to be.

In the Bible, the word, "saint" simply means a person of faith. The great people of faith in the Hebrew scriptures were called saints. In the New Testament, the followers of Jesus were called saints.

If you have read their stories from the Bible, you know that the people in those stories were very much like us. Adam and Eve had the first dysfunctional family. Jacob, whose name was eventually changed to Israel, was a real shyster. He was always trying to get the best of someone. David, the great hero of the Hebrew scriptures, had his human failings, lots of them. Peter, the right hand man of Jesus, was always doing or saying the wrong thing. And Paul had a monumental ego. They were like us.

Yet, they had found their way into a special kind of relationship with God that enabled God to make their lives new and to use them to change the world. What did God do? God enabled them to trust and to love. And that made them saints. Living daily in an open relationship with a living God brought them to life in a new way and put a growing edge on their stories. It turned their lives into adventures and caused them to be people who were always becoming more than they had been in the past.

Think about those people who first became Christians on the Day of Pentecost. A few of them, the disciples and a few others, had some history of a previous relationship with Jesus, maybe for three years, more or less. Most of them had only heard of Jesus. Or maybe they had seen him and heard him teach back home in Galilee or in the temple in Jerusalem. Even those who liked what he said must have known he was a controversial person. After all, he had been crucified by the leaders of their people. Some of them may have even seen it happen.

However, on the Day of Pentecost, there was among the people gathered in Jerusalem a spreading circle of realization that Jesus actually had been sent from God to save them to a new life of faith and love. They realized the God who sent Jesus was still present and at work among them to forgive, to liberate, and to enable them to trust and love. The realization started with those who had known Jesus the longest: the disciples. Then it spread throughout the city. It spread among the people who had come from all over the ancient world to worship on the Jewish feast Day of Passover and who would be returning to all parts of the world to tell what they had experienced. By bedtime, several thousand people had become believers.

It is not likely that many of them went to bed early. Can you imagine how they felt? They must have been caught up in the excitement of a new beginning. The Bible says, "They devoted themselves to the apostles' teaching and fellowship, to the breaking of bread and the prayers" (Acts 2:42). They must have been eager to learn all they could about their new faith and to experience it as deeply as they could through fellowship and worship. They must have known they would soon be scattered in a big world that would not understand them. They must have known they would have to experience their interactions with the risen Christ through their interactions with life, and they would need to know how to recognize what God would be doing in their lives. They must have known they would be called to live lives and take actions that could be dangerous and costly. After all, Jesus was crucified. They needed to learn all they could while they were together.

Their lives of discipleship, and the adventure of living out of a relationship with the living God, did indeed keep them growing. Years later, an older teacher named John wrote to them, "See what love the Father has given us, that we should be called children of God; and that is what we are. The reason the world does not know us is that it did not know him. Beloved, we are God's children now; what we will be has not yet been revealed. What we do know is this: when he is revealed, we will be like him, for we will see him as he is. And all who have this hope in them purify themselves, just as he is pure" (1 John 3:1-3).

John was talking to people who had lived lives shaped by a relationship with God. They had lived that kind of life for many years, under very difficult circumstances. One thing they had been given that they could hang on to was the knowledge that they were children of God. They had received a gift because God loved them. But God's love had continued to work within them and to help them grow in their ability to love. Yes, that's what it's all about. It's about learning to love as God loves — and God makes that happen. Those who hold on to the hope that they will someday be able to love as God loves will keep on working at growing toward it.

That is the shape of the lives of the saints of God. Those people represented by the stone statues we see in cathedrals were real, down-to-earth people in whose lives something very special and exciting happened.

When we think about the great saints of the past, we may wonder, why aren't there any saints today? The answer is, there are. Can you think of any people living today who might be thought of as saints? When we ask, we immediately begin to think of people like Mother Teresa of Calcutta or maybe Martin Luther King Jr. or some other heroes of the faith who stand head and shoulders above the rest of us.

Let me suggest that you look somewhere else. Remember, the saints were real, ordinary people who had entered into a relationship of faith and love with God. Look around you right now. Do you see anyone in this room who fits that description? Do you see some? Look more closely. Do *you* fit that description? Most of us want to "go into orbit" when someone suggests that we can be saints. For one thing, many of us are not at all sure we want to be what the word "saint" suggests to us, someone who is perfect, someone carved out of stone. For another thing, we know ourselves too well. We know that we fall short of being what we ought to be. We are really not sure we want to be expected to live up to any high expectations.

But look again. Most of your families are no bigger messes than Adam's was. Most of you are no more crooked than Jacob or compromised than David or klutzey than Peter or arrogant than Paul. Yes, you are human — but that is one of the qualifications for a saint. Surprise!

There is another qualification. Do you have faith in God? Most of us have neglected our faith and not done much about it except to go to church now and then. But you do have faith in God, don't you? You did make a profession of faith in God at some time in the past, didn't you? And you haven't taken it back, have you? And you are here today for some reason or another. Do you have faith in God, at least a little bit? Jesus said that, if we have faith even as big as a tiny mustard seed, we can do great things.

It is important for you to believe in God. But it is also important — really important — for you to know that God believes in you. Most of us get our images of ourselves from the images of us that others hold. Most of us who have learned to believe in ourselves were able to begin believing in ourselves because someone else believed in us, someone important — like our parents, a brother or sister, a friend, or a spouse. Later, our images of ourselves may have been either reinforced or damaged by our encounters with life. If some experience in life damages our images of ourselves, it is knowing that someone important still believes in us that can help us to recover our belief in ourselves. Those people who believe in us are important. But there is one who believes in us who is the most important one of all. It is God. In the eyes of God, you are a beloved daughter or son, one born to love, one born to be a saint. And God keeps believing in you no matter what life does to you.

What would it take to make you want to claim that heritage? No, we are not talking about the heritage of someone who goes around acting like he is better than other people. The biblical saints didn't act that way. We are talking about someone who at least wants to be able to live in love in all his or her relationships, and maybe someone who would be willing to be used by God to make the world a better place. You may have to wait until you get disillusioned with all of the other little prizes you are scrambling after. But when you finally decide to claim it, the heritage of a saint is there for you.

When you do, you will want to give some attention to rediscovering the heritage that is there for you, the shape of the better life that God is offering you, the things the Bible tells you about the love God has for you, and what God is doing in your life and in your world to make that life possible for you. The best place to do that is in the learning experiences and the worship services and the fellowship of your church… in the fellowship of the saints. Yes, your church. It can do for you what the disciples' fellowship did for those early converts on the Day of Pentecost.

Learn well because, sooner or later, you are going to have to move out and live a different kind of life in a world that does not understand. Sooner or later you are going to feel compelled to try to make a difference in the world that the world really doesn't want to have made. It can be difficult. It can be demanding.

But you don't have to do it alone. The God in whose eyes you are a beloved son or daughter, the God who believes that you can actually be a saint, the God who believes in you is always with you. God is not the only one who is always here believing in you. All of the saints of the past are here with you and pulling for you. They really aren't dead, you know. When they died, they went to be with God. God is here with us — and so are they. We may not have statues of the saints from the past standing in alcoves around our sanctuary, but we don't need them. The real saints are here; Jacob, David, Peter, Paul, and also some others whom you have known, people who loved you and believed in you and wanted what is best for you. Can you name them? They understand your humanity. Oh, yes they do. But they are still believing in you, pulling for you, and hoping that you will choose the heritage of the saints and make the most of it. They, like God, are promising to be here with you as you give it your best try.

In the book of Hebrews, there is a place where the author talks about the presence of the saints. He says: "Therefore, since we are surrounded by so great a cloud of witnesses, let us also lay aside every weight and the sin that clings so closely, and let us run with perseverance the race that is set before us, looking to Jesus the pioneer and perfecter of our faith..." (Hebrews 12:1-2a). Amen.

Proper 27
Pentecost 25
Ordinary Time 32
1 Thessalonians 4:13-18

What Can We Believe about the End of Time?

Today we are going to talk about one of the biggest puzzles in the study of the Bible. What can we believe about the end of time? For Paul and the early Christians in Thessalonica that was no puzzle at all. They knew exactly what they believed about the end of time. "The Lord himself, with a cry of command, with the archangel's call and the sound of God's trumpet, will descend from heaven, and the dead in Christ will rise first. Then we who are alive, who are left, will be caught up in the clouds together with them to meet the Lord in the air; and so we will be with the Lord forever" (vv. 16-17). There was also an expectation that the Lord would bring in a new era of peace and justice on earth.

This is what is called the apocalyptical expectation. It was widespread among the Jewish people during the time of Jesus. The Essene people, who gave us the Dead Sea Scrolls, were completely caught up in this way of thinking. It was a part of the way in which the Jews saw reality. It became very much a part of the beliefs of the early church. They expected some special things to happen when the Messiah came. Then Jesus, the Messiah, came and died and was raised from the dead, but the new order did not come. The people were confused. Then the early Christians came to believe that Jesus was coming again to finish his work. They expected it to happen soon.

Since this letter was the earliest thing written that became part of the New Testament, it shows the shape of the faith of the earliest church. The belief that Jesus was coming again soon was a part of the faith of the Thessalonian Christians. They thought it would happen in their life time. That theme is scattered throughout the New Testament. It is hard to study the Bible without tripping over it again and again.

But it didn't happen. Time kept going on and it hasn't happened yet. So what can we believe about it?

There are some people who sincerely believe that we should still live expecting Jesus to return at any time and bring history to an end. From time to time, some little sect of people emerges who believe that they know the exact time when Jesus will return. As the date approaches, they abandon their lives in this world and get ready to meet the Lord. But it hasn't happened yet. From time to time, someone will write a sensational book based on a literal interpretation of things the Bible says about the end of time and it will become a best seller. There is a school of theological thought called, "dispensationalism," which takes those expectations literally and seriously. Some of its followers even get involved in promoting political action that is intended to hasten the return of Christ. We are all familiar with the popular series of fictional books called the "Left Behind" series that are based on this way of thinking.

Most of us see that almost 2,000 years have passed since the early church expected Christ to return. So we have decided not to organize our lives around the belief that history as we know it is about to come to an end. But, if we can't believe that, what are we to make of all of the scriptural references to this theme? What can we believe about it?

We can get some guidance from reading the rest of the New Testament. As we do that, we will discover the early church, including Paul himself, gradually began to realize Christ was not going to return as soon as they thought he would. We can learn from the things they did with their beliefs about the end of time.

First, when the early Christians became aware that the end of time was not coming soon, they realized they had to get ready to live a while longer in this world. At the time when Paul wrote to the Thessalonians, the church had very little organizational structure. The apostles were the leaders and there were also some natural leaders that emerged in each congregation. By the time he wrote 1 Corinthians 12, structures of congregational life were emerging. By the time the letters to Timothy and Titus were written, something like an ordained ministry was emerging. They were getting organized for the long haul. They also started writing books intended to pass on the memories of Jesus and the witness of the early Christians to future generations. The four gospels, and the book of Acts, and probably even Paul's letter to the Romans were written for that purpose. They were getting ready to stay a while — and so should we.

We need to organize our lives, and the life of our church, as if we will be living in this world for a number of years, probably a large number of years, and as if we will be participating in human history that is likely to go on for generations to come. That is important. God is at work in our lives and in our world today. We should not let our religion drift off into some spiritual clouds. We are called to live each day of this life as an interaction with God. And God calls us to find ways to serve him by participating in the work that God is doing in this world. But the apocalyptical way of thinking leaves us some valuable lessons we ought to hold on to.

In the passage we have read today, Paul gives the Thessalonians some assurance about those who had died. There was a widespread belief among the Jewish people during the days of Jesus, held by most of the early Christians, that there would be a day of general resurrection. There is a belief all of the saints who have died will wait for one great day of resurrection when all of the dead will rise at once.

In some other parts of the Bible, we find a belief that those who die will be raised immediately after their death and go directly to be with the Lord. As Jesus was dying on the cross, he said to the man who was dying on a cross next to his, "Truly I tell you, today you will be with me in Paradise" (Luke 23:43).

This assurance reminds us of something we sometimes try to forget. Whether or not time is about to come to an end for the world, there will come a time when time will come to an end for each of us. Someday each of us is going to die. Most of us try to deal with that reality by not thinking about it. We like to pretend that we will live forever. Then when someone close to us dies and the shape of reality forces itself into our consciousness, we have a hard time dealing with it. The truth is that we are all mortal. We are all going to die sometime. That is part of who we are. There is a better way of dealing with that than pretending it isn't so or living in dread of it. Our faith invites us to see our mortality in the context of God's immortality.

The important thing for us to remember is that the God who has given us being, the God who has shown himself to us in Jesus Christ, is eternal. The one thing we need to know when our loved ones die, or when we think about the time when we will die, is that the God who loves us will be there beyond this life to receive us. The one who raised Jesus up from death to life can raise us up too. The when, where, and how are not important. The important thing for us to remember is that, beyond this life, we go to be with God. That is a belief that we can hold on to. And that hope will make a difference in the quality of our lives here in this world.

By the time Paul wrote his last letter, the letter to the Romans, he had stopped talking so much about the return of Christ. (By the way, theologians sometimes refer to the return of Christ as the "parousia.") He had evidently come to believe that it would happen some time in the distant future. But Paul still believed that we are living between two ages, an old age of temporary and unimportant and sometimes bad things that is passing away, and a new age that is dawning, an age of things that are eternal.

If you will look around, you will find that is a pretty good way of making sense of the things you will see. There are things that seem like they are made of tickey tackey, things that have no lasting substance or real meaning. Those things make demands upon us, and sometimes we have to put up with them. Unfortunately, some people choose to build their lives on them. There are other things that are real, of lasting importance and genuine substance. Paul would say that those are the things that are of the age to come, God's new age.

This is something that is relevant to our lives. All of us, especially the younger ones of us, make decisions about what we are going to allow to be important to us. We decide what we are going to build our lives out of. Like the three little pigs building their houses, some of us decide to build our lives of flimsy, ephemeral things like material prosperity, social prominence, and shallow pleasure. Others choose to build lives out of things of eternal significance, like loving relationships and commitments to great purposes and enjoyment of the real beauty of life.

Paul says we should live our lives, insofar as we can, in accordance with the age to come. We will still have to put up with the things that belong to the age that is passing away. But we should try hard not to let those things become too important to us. We should try, as best we can, to build our lives of the things that belong to the age to come, things like goodness, justice, beauty, and love. You will find that way of thinking reflected in Paul's letter to the Romans in chapter 8. This is a good way of putting your life together. It is one to the good things we can learn from the biblical teachings about the end of time.

John, and the Christians who were associated with him, began to see the time of an ultimate reckoning with God in a different way. They began to see judgment and repentance and the beginning of eternal life, not as something that is going to happen at the end of time, but as something that can happen whenever we encounter the risen Christ. That can happen here and now, right in the middle of your daily life experiences, whenever you become aware that God is dealing with you through your interactions with life.

Believing that can fill your everyday life with expectancy. John teaches us to take the things that the Bible teaches us about the end of time and let them interpret for us the meaning of the things that are happening in each moment of our present time.

That is a very good way to interpret the book of Revelation. The book of Revelation is the biggest and most impressive piece of apocalyptical literature in the New Testament. In every generation, there have been people who have taken the book of Revelation literally, as a description of the count down leading to the end of time. That is what it appears to be. But, in fact, it is an example of a kind of literature that the Jews and early Christians used to encourage people who were living under oppression.

The writer of the book of Revelation was a leader of the church in Asia Minor during a time of persecution. He was arrested by the Roman authorities and, because he refused to renounce his faith, his property was confiscated and he was confined to a prison camp on the island of Patmos. While he was there, he worried about his fellow Christians back on the mainland who were threatened with a fate like his or worse. He wanted to write something to encourage them. He adopted a form of literature that the Jewish people had used in similar circumstances. He used highly symbolic language to escape censorship. If you want to know how this works, listen to a recording of the once popular song, "Bye, bye

Miss American Pie."[1] If you were a teenager when that song first came out, you would recognize the meaning of all of the highly symbolic images it strings together. If you are from another generation, it is bewildering.

The message of the book is simply this. Tyrants have come and gone in the past. This tyrant, the Roman Empire, will go like the rest. So hang in there. Keep your faith. The future is in God's hands. Ultimately, you will be on the winning side. That is something we can believe. And that belief can give you courage whether you are being oppressed by a political tyrant, an abusive relationship, or a case of depression.

A pastor went to visit a lady who was hospitalized because of a nervous break down. She was a highly motivated person who was dealing with some very demanding situations in life and they had gotten the best of her. The first few times the pastor went by, the lady was sedated. Then finally one day he found her awake and alert. She said, "Pastor I am glad to see you. I've been reading the Bible." The pastor thought, "Good. That is just what she needs: large doses of the twenty-third Psalm." But when he asked what she had been reading, she said she was reading the book of Revelation. The pastor swallowed hard and began to try to explain that she should not let the drastic images in the apocalypse upset her. The lady said, "Oh, no. I have found it a great source of peace." She had heard the real message of the book, and in fact, it is very similar to the message of the twenty-third Psalm.

It may be hard for us to believe that the Bible's vivid images of the last days are descriptions of something that is actually going to happen, at least not any time soon. But we ought not to tear those pages out of our Bibles. Like great works of art and literature, they bear witness to something that can add rich meaning to our lives. There are lots of things in those images that we can believe if we have the courage to claim them. And if we do, our lives will be much better for it. Amen.

1. Don McLean, "American Pie" (Los Angeles, United Artists Records, UAST-7879-A-RE10).

Proper 28
Pentecost 26
Ordinary Time 33
1 Thessalonians 5:1-11

What Can We Believe about Judgment Day?

Most of the biblical images of the coming day of the Lord suggest a belief that it will be a day of judgment, a day when everyone will appear before the judgment seat of God and be judged and sent either to heaven or to hell. That is probably the most unattractive feature of Christian tradition for believers and the thing most likely to "turn off" outsiders. It calls to mind images of preachers thundering judgmental messages from their pulpits, trying to generate guilty feelings and to scare people into making a profession of faith with the threat of hellfire. Almost as unattractive are those neighbors, coworkers, or family members who are always measuring everyone by their own standards of righteousness and criticizing or rejecting those who do not measure up. Judgment, understood in these ways, is certainly not very attractive.

Yet, the Bible does have much to say about judgment. What can we believe about the judgment of God? You may want to ask, "Do we have to believe anything about it?" The answer is "yes." Judgment does play a role in the Christian faith. But it is very important for us to understand what judgment is and what role it plays.

First, we need to understand that there is a difference between judgment and condemnation. It is hard to see the difference when we are talking about a last judgment. But we are going to see that judgment takes place in some other contexts too. In those situations, the difference is significant.

Condemnation is a death sentence. It is usually thought of as final. But judgment is a wake up call. It is something done by someone who loves you to help you recognize that you are in trouble, and you need to make some changes.

Let me import a little bit of John's teaching into this study of Paul's letter. John wrote, "Indeed, God did not send his Son into the world to condemn the world, but in order that the world might be saved through him" (John 3:17). A little later, he wrote, "And this is judgment, that the light has come into the world, and people loved darkness rather than light because their deeds were evil" (John 3:19). This is an example of John taking things written about the last days and letting them interpret the meaning of things that are happening every day. In John's gospel, we read many stories about Jesus confronting people, pushing them to recognize all that was wrong in their lives, offering them a better possibility, and inviting them to make needed changes. That is judgment. It is not condemnation. It is something done by someone who loves you and who wants something better for you.

There is a practice that is sometimes used to help problem drinkers break the hold of alcoholism on their lives that is a lot like that kind of judgment. Quite often, an alcoholic is able to convince himself that he doesn't really have a drinking problem, even though everyone around him may see that his life is falling apart. That is called denial. Some alcoholics are really good at it. They may construct elaborate explanations for everything that is going wrong and even persuade some people who are close to them that everything is all right.

To break that pattern of denial, some people who really care about the alcoholic person may stage a meeting between the alcoholic and certain important other people, family members, employer, friends, and people injured by his alcoholism. They may have to trick the alcoholic into coming to the meeting. The people may be assembled in the alcoholic's living room when he comes home. Then, one by one, they will lovingly but without equivocation, confront the alcoholic with the evidence that there is a serious problem and with the consequences that will follow if he does not change. His daughter may tell him very plainly how embarrassed she was when her friends saw him drunk and tell him that she does not ever want him to be around her friends again. An employer may catalog the times when his drinking has interfered with his work and then tell him that he will lose his job if there is not a change. His wife may list the ways in which his drinking has injured her and the family and tell him that she will definitely leave him if he does not change. The people who stage the confrontation will have already made arrangements for him to leave immediately to get therapy. Then the alcoholic will see that he has a decision to make, and he will understand clearly what is at stake. That is judgment. It cannot be a pleasant experience. But it is something done in love and it may save the life of the person for whom it is done.

Paul must have been very familiar with that kind of judgment. He always remembered the day when he was a zealous young Pharisee, full of ambition and hatred, who was traveling to Damascus to persecute the early Christians. On the way, he was confronted by the risen Christ who said, "Saul, what are you doing? Why are you persecuting me?" That brought him up short and forced him to reckon with his own wrongness. It is important to recognize what happened next. God did not pack him off to hell. Instead, God sent a brave little man named Ananius around to tell him about God's forgiving love and to inform him that God had something important for him to do. That is judgment.

Judgment can sneak up on us and surprise us. Paul spoke of judgment day coming at a time when no one expects it. He was talking about the last judgment. But we can have individual experiences of judgment like Paul's at any time.

Any day can be the day of the Lord, the day of our ultimate reckoning with God.

Judgment day may come to you when some situation in life calls you to live up to your highest possibility as a person. Some crisis arises that calls for decisive action. Some neighbor has a need that you could meet. Some great issue of truth or justice needs an advocate and you know you could step up and say what needs to be said. You are the one — or one of the ones — who could act and make a difference. But doing what needs to be done may be dangerous or costly. The risen Christ often comes to us in situations like that and calls us to make a loving and courageous response. You have a decision to make.

Paul suggests that if you are wide awake and "living in the light," you will be ready to make the right response. If you have drifted off into the kind of complacency that often overtakes us, you may not. If you find that you did not have the love or the courage needed to make the response that your humanity requires, you may find yourself under judgment. You may have to reckon with the knowledge that you did not live up to your best possibility.

Things can get even more complicated. If you do try to make the loving and courageous response that life calls for, you may find yourself involved in conflict. You may find yourself having to make some kind of compromise to act decisively. A good example of the kind of situation in which that can happen is when you feel called to become involved in politics. Even if you try hard to do what you believe is right, you may come out feeling compromised and beaten and not good.

What happens then? Are you condemned to go to hell for your shortcomings? No, it is interesting to notice that neither Paul nor John ever says anything about hell. Some of the other Bible writers do. The fact that neither Paul nor John ever say anything about it suggests that hell is not nearly as important a part of the Christian understanding of things as we have sometimes thought. So, if hell is not the next stop, what is? Paul tells us. "God has destined us not for wrath but for obtaining salvation through our Lord Jesus Christ, who died for us, so that whether we are awake or asleep we may live with him" (vv. 9-10). Any real serious engagement with life is likely to bring us into the experience of judgment. And that experience will make us aware that we stand in need of the saving grace of God. It makes us realize that we are made able to stand in the presence of God, our judge, not by our own goodness, but by the forgiving love of God. We are helped to realize who we really are. We are sinners accepted by God because of his forgiving love for us. The sooner we learn to know ourselves in that way, the sooner we will be ready to move on to the next step.

Yes, there is another step. If we are honest with God about what needs to be fixed in our lives, and open to the loving work of God in our lives, God will work with us to help us become all that we can be.

Paul urged the Thessalonians to equip themselves to meet the times of trial by "staying awake and sober" and by putting on the breastplate of faith and love and the helmet of the hope of salvation. He told the members of the church to "encourage each one another and build up each other" (vv. 6-11). Judgment is an important part of the process that can lead us to fullness of life and that can lead the world to salvation.

In fact, the experience of living under judgment can become a part of the self-understanding of a truly mature person. Sometimes we put much too much emphasis on innocence. When we seek someone to trust with a responsibility or with leadership, we tend to look for someone who has never done anything wrong. The problem with that is most of the people who have never done anything wrong are people who have never done anything. In a world where so much needs to be done, never doing anything is doing something wrong. Don't misunderstand. There is no virtue in doing wrong. We should always try as hard as we can to do what is right. Anyone who tries to live decisively in this world of ambiguities will inevitably wind up doing some things that are at least partially wrong. In that situation, it is important to be aware of the judgment that rests upon even our best actions. That will keep us realistic about ourselves and about the things we are trying to do.

Many of the great leaders in the Bible were people who had been through the experience of judgment, repentance, and renewal so often that it became a part of their understanding of who they were and how they stood in the presence of God. Indeed, it seems that experience can equip a person for leadership. Think of Jacob, Moses, and David.

The same is true of many of the great people in history. People who are familiar with the history of the state of Texas will know the name Sam Houston. Sam Houston was the general who led a rag-tag group of pioneers in a battle that defeated the Mexican army and won the independence of Texas and several other states. He was the first president of the Republic of Texas and, after Texas became one of the United States, he served both as governor and as United States senator. He was truly a hero. He demonstrated the depth of his heroism by sacrificing all he had gained by courageously taking a stand for something he believed. He spoke out opposing the secession of Texas during the Civil War.

Sam Houston was not an innocent person. He was a maverick. In his youth, he withdrew for a while from his prominent Southern family to live among the Cherokees. Later, after becoming a hero in the war against the Creek Indians, he was elected governor of Tennessee at a very young age. Then he made the devastating discovery that his young bride loved another man. He resigned his office and withdrew again to live among the Cherokees. There he earned another Cherokee name that meant "The big drunk."

He eventually moved to the frontier territory of Texas, got his life together, and became the heroic person he is remembered to be. In the process, he was baptized. For him, that must have represented a real experience of repentance and renewal. He always remained a maverick. Having come through the experiences of judgment and renewal must have actually equipped him to give the leadership he eventually gave. How many other heroes of history can you think of for whom the experience of judgment was a part of their preparation? Of how many of your own heroes is that true?

I am tempted to sign off by wishing you a happy judgment day. But that would be foolish. No one can enjoy the experience of standing under judgment. It is like having surgery — or like having a bad tooth extracted. But I can wish you a happy day after judgment day. That is a real possibility. And you can believe that. Amen.

Christ the King
Proper 29
Ephesians 1:15-23

What Can We Believe about the Reign of Christ?

    The church calendar says that this is the day on which we celebrate the festival of Christ the King. That makes this a very important day. The idea of the kingdom of God, or the kingdom of Christ, is one of the most important biblical and theological explanations of the meaning of the Christian faith. It probably represents the very heart of Jesus' own teachings. Mark tells us that right after Jesus returned from being tempted in the wilderness, "Jesus came to Galilee, proclaiming the good news of God, and saying, 'The time is fulfilled, and the kingdom of God has come near; repent, and believe the good news' " (Mark 1:14-15). Later, the writer of the letter to the Ephesians gave a more universalistic interpretation to that concept. He says that "with all wisdom and insight he has made known to us the mystery of his will, according to his good pleasure that he set forth in Christ, as a plan for the fullness of time, to gather up all things in him, things in heaven and things on earth" (Ephesians 1:8-10). Later, he wrote that God has put his great power to work in Christ "when he raised him from the dead and seated him at his right hand in the heavenly places, far above all rule and authority and power and dominion, and above every name that is named, not only in this age but in the age to come. And he has put all things under his feet and has made him the head over all things for the church, which is his body, the fullness of him who fills all in all" (vv. 20-23). This passage elaborates on the concept of the kingdom of God by picturing God and Jesus in the splendor of all powerful rulers over all things.

It certainly is an awesome image. But, if we think much about it, most of us won't like that image very much. We don't know an awful lot about kings, and we really don't like what we do know about them. Those of us who are Americans remember that our country came into existence by being in a war fought to get rid of a king. We don't much like the idea of anyone playing the role of a king in our lives, not even Christ. And the non-Christian peoples of the world have a problem with all of our talk about Christ being the all powerful king of the whole creation. To them that sounds like a rationale for Christian countries conquering them and forcing our religion and our way of life on them. The truth is at times in history, Christians did think that way. There are some problems with the image. But, the meaning behind the image is very important and valuable to all of us. Let's try to catch a vision of the meaning. What can we believe about Christ the king and about the kingdom of God?

For people in biblical days, there was always a king. The king was the most important other in their lives. The strength and effectiveness of the king determined the well being of the people of the realm. The way in which the king chose to rule determined the quality of life in the kingdom. If the king was a cruel tyrant, as so many of them were, the people lived in fear. The expectations of the king were the responsibilities of the people. The people's relationship with the king shaped their lives.

Is there any "other" that plays a role like that in our lives or in our world? That question may set us all to squinting and thinking hard. Most of us probably want to say, "I can't think of anything that is so important that my relationship with it shapes my life." We have separate relationships with different "others" and they all have different effects on our lives. Think now, can you imagine all those separate realities forming one big other reality whose relationship with you determines how you live? Can you see yourself having a relationship with reality as a whole? Can you see yourself living in relationship with life? We do sometimes see ourselves living in some kind of a relationship with life, don't we? The shape of that relationship determines the quality of our lives.

Now let's take one more step. Can you imagine one great reality, a living reality, standing behind that reality that we experience as "life" and relating to us in all of our interactions with life? Can you imagine that the greater reality that is out there relating to you in all of your interactions with life is God? Can you? Maybe your honest answer will be "no." You may never have thought of God in that way. And you may be having trouble getting this picture into focus. If you can't get this picture right now, that's all right. Just stay with us until you see the whole picture. Then you can make a decision about it. The point is the Bible writers compared God, and the risen Christ as an aspect of God, to a king in order to say they play the role in our lives of that all important other whose interactions with us shape our lives.

Now, if we do live in relationship with some great other, that relationship will ultimately shape our lives. We can learn how that works by remembering how the lives and personalities of children are shaped. They are shaped mostly through their interactions with the most important others in their lives: their parents. How the child experiences his or her parents and how they interact can make a big difference. Let's make up a case study to see how this works.

Imagine a little boy who is being raised by a single parent who is seriously addicted to narcotics. The parent's way of relating to the child varies between being neglectful and being abusive. The parent often stays gone for days at a time leaving the child with nothing to eat. When the parent comes in, the child has to hide to avoid being beaten. On the rare occasion when the parent is sober, the parent talks about how much he or she loves the child, but the child really can't figure out what that means. It only confuses him. If that kind of a relationship with the most important other shapes the child's life, what shape is that child's life likely to take?

Now imagine one day, the child welfare people come and take the child away. At first the child is terrified because he is being taken away from all that he knows. The child is taken to a group home for children. Eventually the child comes to realize that he is safe here and there is plenty to eat. The people who care for him are kind, but no one treats him like he is special. The child has the idea that this arrangement is temporary and he can't imagine what is ahead for him. If this is the shape of the child's relationship with the important other, what effect is it likely to have on his life?

Now imagine one day, a man and a woman come to the group home and the child is told that these people have come to adopt him. They will be his new parents. Again, the child is frightened. But eventually the child realizes that these people are relating to him as no one ever has before. They show him a room they say is his room. They call him to supper. They ask him what he likes to eat and what he wants to be when he grows up. They spend time playing with him and they seem to enjoy it. They take him to school and they talk with the teacher about him. When he gets sick at school, they leave work and come to get him. When he acts up, they punish him, but they don't hurt him and, when it is all over, everything is okay again. After a year of this, the child begins to understand what love means. If the child's life is being shaped by that kind of a relationship with the most important other, what shape is the child's life likely to take?

Who the most important other is in a person's life, and what kind of relationship a person has with that most important other, can make a big difference in the shape and quality of a person's life, can't it? If that is true, it is awfully important for us to know something about that great other in interaction with which we live our lives. We need to know what — or who — it is and how it relates to us and how we ought to respond to it. Many of us just drift into some kind of a relationship with life that is shaped by our good and bad experiences. We may or may not put together any kind of an image of who or what that is out there that keeps coming to meet us in life. Christians believe that Jesus came to show us who it is that is meeting us and interacting with us in all of our experiences of life. Jesus came to show us how that other relates to us and how we can best relate to the other so that our lives can take the best shape possible. Is this all coming together now?

Jesus came to show us that there is someone who really is the most important other out there, someone who is greater than all of the little tyrants that keep trying to get us to let them be king of our lives. There is someone who really does play the role of the king. And that one who really is the great other is someone who loves us and cares about our well being, and is even willing to make costly commitments to our lives. That other invites us to respond to him — and to life — in basic trust and love and to allow trust and love to shape our lives. The one who made himself known to us through Jesus Christ is still God. The one who lived among us to make God known has become an aspect of the God who meets us in life day by day. That can get a little complicated. Just hold on to this. The Bible writers talk about Christ being the king in order to tell us that the most important other in our world and in our lives is someone who loves us and is working for our salvation just like Jesus did. Can you imagine what shape our lives might take if we really allow that great other to play the role of king in our lives?

The idea of the kingdom of God and of Christ has other dimensions too. We have to stretch a little more. We have seen that the image of the kingdom of God is a way of talking about our personal relationship with God. It is also a way of talking about the shape of all reality and a way of talking about the future toward which God is moving the creation.

God is not just our little personal God. Yes, we each have a very personal and intimate relationship with God. That is not to say we can have a relationship with God but rather that we each do have a relationship with God. We all live in daily interaction with God, whether we realize it or not. We make decisions about how we will respond and relate to God and to life and that determines the quality of our lives. The very same kind of interaction is going on between God and every other person on the face of the earth. God is reaching out to each of us in love and inviting each of us to respond in trust and love. That gives a special kind of unity to the human race, doesn't it? Stretch a little more. That greater reality in relationship with whom we live our daily lives is the one who created the world. And out beyond the atmosphere of our little planet is a reality so vast that our most brilliant scientists have not yet been able to imagine its dimensions. We have to believe that all of that is part of the reality that exists in the realm of the God whom we are invited to call king. All of that is the creation of someone who loves us, someone who loves us all.

We can spend a lot of time thinking through the implications of all that. One of the first implications that will emerge is if God loves us all, God must want us to love one another. Jesus said he does. That is really pretty basic. But what a great difference it would make if we took that seriously. When we get that picture, it will be very clear that believing Christ is the king will never give anyone an excuse to try to conquer and suppress anyone else. On the contrary, it will mean that we ought to be busy loving each other and being committed to the well being of all people just like God is. That gives us a promising image of the end toward which

God is trying to move the whole creation. That makes sense of the words from Ephesians that speak of God's "plan for the fullness of time, to gather up all things in him, things in heaven and things on earth" (v. 10).

During the 1960s, a certain musical drama was presented that was based on the "Hippie" way of life. It was called "Hair."[1] For several good reasons, you don't often hear it referred to in church. There was one song in that musical that foretells and celebrates the dawning of a new age when peace and love would govern everything, even the movement of the planets and the stars. Remember? It was called "The Age of Aquarius." That kind of expectancy was not new. Ever since the letter to the Ephesians was written — or before — Christians have believed that a new age of peace and love is coming. That expectancy has given Christians something to celebrate, a hope to hold on to, something in which to commit themselves, and a new way to live their lives. But that new age Christians have expected is not the age of Aquarius, it is the kingdom of God, the reign of Christ the king.

This series of sermons is designed to peel away some of the wrappings of the Christian faith in which we can no longer believe and show us the important things that we can still believe. This one ends in a somewhat different place. I hope that we have shown you an image of the meaning of the idea that Christ is king that will make sense in terms of our modern way of thinking. But this time, instead of saying, "Here is something you can still believe," I have to say, "Can you believe this?" Can you believe that there is a greater reality out there relating to you and to every other person through our interactions with daily life and that great other is someone who loves us and wants us to live in love? It will take great imagination and great courage to actually believe that and to let that belief shape your life. If you can believe it, you can experience life in an entirely new way. You can experience the new life of the kingdom of God. Amen.

1. "Hair. The American Tribal Love-Rock Musical." James Rado, Gerome Ragin, Galt McDermit, first presented off-Broadway, 1967.

Thanksgiving
2 Corinthians 9:6-15

What Can We Believe about Stuff?

Today we celebrate the festival of Thanksgiving. Today we remember and celebrate all that we should be thankful for. Goodness knows, we have a lot, life, love, freedom, so many intangible blessings. But very often, when we decide to list the things we have to be thankful for, we think first about — well — things, the material things we have, stuff. Stuff is very important to many of us, maybe too important, so important that we get antsy when we think the pastor is about to preach a stewardship sermon. Sure enough, right here in the midst of our thanksgiving celebration, we find ourselves reading a scripture lesson in which Paul is preaching a stewardship sermon. He is preparing to take up an offering for the relief of needy Christians in Jerusalem. If you read all of chapter 6, you get the idea that Paul has taken lessons from the same people who taught the fund-raisers who call you on the telephone asking you to support various charities. Paul really knows how to "make an ask" and to apply the pressure.

Well, what about our stuff? Where does it fit into the life of faith? What can we believe about stuff? The Bible actually has quite a lot to say about it.

Much of what the Bible says about stuff has to do with the problems that stuff can cause for us. The problems are not really with the stuff itself but rather with the ways in which we choose to relate ourselves to it and the roles we allow stuff to play in our lives. Stuff is tangible. We can see it and touch it. We know that it can do good things for us.

So we are always tempted to rely on it and to put our trust in it. Given the choice between trusting the intangible promise that God will provide and trusting money in the bank, we have a hard time doing what we know a good Christian ought to do. When we put our trust in stuff, we naturally begin to be obedient to the demands that stuff makes upon us. To paraphrase an old hymn, what we trust, we also obey. So, many of us have drifted into a life that is organized primarily around getting, keeping, and managing stuff.

This is nothing new. It is at least as old as the Exodus. The people of Israel had a hard time persuading themselves to leave Egypt and to venture into the wilderness following the God who promised to make of them a great nation. They were slaves in Egypt. But at least they had some stuff. They had a place to sleep and food to eat. They were very reluctant to risk leaving that. And when they finally did arrive in their promised land, they had to work hard at holding on to their religious heritage that emphasized justice and human dignity because the people among whom they came to live followed a very attractive religion that focused on material prosperity. That is really what the worship of Baal and the other fertility cults was all about.

Today, we live in a materialistic culture that teaches values very much like those of the ancient fertility cults. It identifies wealth with well being, encourages jealousy, makes a virtue of greed, teaches us to evaluate everyone, including ourselves, in terms of how much stuff we have, and, in many ways, makes us miserable when we should be happy.

Jesus summed up the problem. He said, "No one can serve two masters... You cannot serve God and wealth" (Matthew 6:24). Jesus then went on to explain that you have to put your trust in God so you can be free to be obedient to God. "Therefore do not worry, saying, 'What will we eat?' or 'What will we drink?' or 'What will we wear?' ... indeed your heavenly Father knows that you need all these things.

But strive first for the kingdom of God and his righteousness, and all these things will be given to you as well" (Matthew 6:31-33). In our scripture reading for today, Paul emphasizes that the Corinthians will have to learn to trust God to provide in order to gain the freedom to give. You have to make a decision about where you will put your trust and what will be your primary commitment. You have to let that decision shape your life.

Having lots of stuff has been a problem for lots of people. There was a time when some Christians thought the only way to live a Christian life was to get rid of all of their stuff and move out into the desert and live a monastic life. Even today, there are some who are choosing to live a more simple life. There is a story in the Bible about a wealthy, young man who came to Jesus asking what he would have to do to have eternal life. Jesus appreciated the fact that the young man had actually been trying to live a good life but he saw that he had a problem. His stuff was too important to him. So he said, "Sell all that you own and distribute the money to the poor, and you will have treasures in heaven; then come, follow me" (Luke 18:22). The young man couldn't bring himself to do it. Jesus shook his head sadly and said, "How hard it is for those who have wealth to enter the kingdom of God! Indeed, it is easier for a camel to go through the eye of a needle than for someone who is rich to enter the kingdom of God" (Luke 18:24-25). The disciples, who were still caught up in the notion that rich people can do anything said, "If the rich people can't do it, who can?" Jesus put everything into perspective. "What is impossible for mortals is possible for God" (Luke 18:27). It is not wealth that makes life all that life can be. But if a rich person can stand apart from his or her wealth and relate to God on the same basis as anyone else, then God can work the miracle of salvation in his or her life as well as in any other person's life.

Stuff can be a problem. And yet — and yet — this stuff is part of what God created and called good (Genesis 1:31). We are perfectly right to think of our stuff when we think about the things for which we should be thankful. In fact, we would be very wise to learn to be thankful for what we have.

Our culture of greed has taught us to mouth the myth that says, "No one has ever given me anything. I have earned everything I have by my own hard work and ingenuity and I don't owe anyone anything." Really? The ability to work and circumstances under which we can enjoy the fruit of our work are really extraordinary gifts. There are millions of people in our world, who work harder than we do and whom God loves as much as God loves us, who are living in terrible poverty because of circumstances that are no fault of their own. Why can't we simply accept the fact that, if we have enough, we are very fortunate and be grateful? Gratitude is a form of happiness. Why can't we just let ourselves swap our greedy pride for a liberated happiness and enjoy what we have been given?

Then what does a grateful person do with his or her stuff? There are several things that are appropriate.

First, take charge of what has been given to you. Have it. Don't let it have you. It is easy to become so anxious about the possibility of not having enough that we begin to hoard what we have. We are not really free to use it. We don't really have it. It has us. Of course we should manage what we have well and live within our income. If we can believe that the one who gave us what we have for today will give us what we need for tomorrow, we will be able to possess things in freedom; not in anxiety. Paul made this clear in our scripture lesson for today. "He who supplies seed to the sower and bread for food will supply and multiply your seed for sowing and increase the harvest of your righteousness" (v. 10). Now, some people have taken this idea to extremes, teaching and believing that God will miraculously give us anything we want. You don't have to look at that long to realize that is a matter of trying to make God serve our culture of greed. We must manage responsibly all that is given to us. But if we can do that within an attitude of basic trust, then we can manage it in freedom.

So here you are with some good stuff in your hands. What do you do with it? Use it. Use it to provide for the needs of your family. Use it to enlarge the perimeters of your own life. Use it for educational opportunities that will strengthen and enable your personhood and that of those near you. Enjoy it. Make the most of it. Let it make your life good.

Some of the stuff you have may become sacramental. Jesus took common things, bread, wine, water, and made them symbols of God's love for us. Some of the things we have will eventually accumulate meanings. They will call to mind loving relationships or memories of happy times. In fact, everything we have can become a reminder of God's love for us. That is why we return thanks before eating meals. It is a good thing to let our stuff become reminders of God's love.

Finally, a loving person who possesses his or her stuff in freedom, will eventually feel a need to share. The needs of your church and your community will naturally become a part of your family budget. These are really not even forms of giving. They are simply uses of your stuff to meet your own needs and those of others around you. When you realize that you are more able than some others to contribute to those shared endeavors, it will be natural for you to share more. If you are really — really — not as able as others to share, you should not feel bad about giving what is appropriate within your means. (Save your guilty feelings for the really bad things that you do.)

There is another claim that loving people cannot ignore. We live in a world in which there are millions of people who live on the verge of starvation. Even in our own communities there are people who, through no fault of their own, do not have enough. That was really the kind of situation that prompted Paul to write what he wrote about sharing. There were Christian brothers and sisters in need back in Judea. The more financially able people in the churches in Greece would naturally want to help. When we catch a vision of the amount of deep human need there is in this world, we will want to include the needs of others in our management of our stuff. What we share will truly become sacramental. As Paul said, "Each of you must give as you have made up your mind, not reluctantly or under compulsion, for God loves a cheerful giver" (v. 7). There is no promise that you will get richer because you share some of your stuff. But knowing that you have made a compassionate response to the needs of some of God's children will bring a satisfaction that will truly enrich your life.

Stuff does play a role in our lives. God planned it that way. It is just awfully important to learn how to live in a right relationship with our stuff. In 2008, Hurricane Ike struck the upper Gulf coast of Texas. The storm surge did an huge amount of damage. The city of Galveston and many other coastal communities were devastated. Fortunately, most people heeded the warning to evacuate and the loss of life was minimal. But the loss of stuff was enormous. The city of Bridge City, Texas, which had about 3,500 homes in it had only fifteen houses that were not flooded. Most of the houses had from three to four feet of sea water in them. Many people lost everything they owned. The people were forced to learn a new relationship with their stuff. They were forced to see themselves separate from their stuff. They grieved the loss of those things that had become sacramental to them, wedding pictures, gifts from loved ones, things with memories attached. But many learned to trust that the one who had provided in the past would again provide in the future. They were grateful for what they had left; life and loved ones. They affirmed the future and got ready to move to meet it with courage. People living nearby could see the great human need of their neighbors and shared their resources and their efforts to help the people of Bridge City and the other devastated communities clean up and make a fresh start.

The storm was a harsh teacher. Hopefully the rest of us can learn more gently how to relate to our stuff, how to receive it gratefully as a gift of God, how to possess it in freedom, how to enjoy it and use it to genuinely enrich and enable our lives, and how to gladly share it with those who have need. Amen.

www.ingramcontent.com/pod-product-compliance
Lightning Source LLC
Chambersburg PA
CBHW071737040426
42446CB00012B/2388